everyday
kindness

everyday kindness

----

365 WAYS TO A PEACEFUL LIFE

An Hachette UK Company
www.hachette.co.uk

First published in 2017 by Pyramid,
an imprint of Octopus Publishing Group Ltd
Carmelite House
50 Victoria Embankment
London, EC4Y 0DZ
www.octopusbooks.co.uk

ISBN: 978-0-7537-3269-4

A CIP catalogue record for this book is available
from the British Library

Printed and bound in China

10 9 8 7 6 5 4 3 2

Publisher: Lucy Pessell
Designer: Lisa Layton
Design: Ummagumma
Contributing Editor: Emma Hill
Editor: Sarah Vaughan
Production Controller: Beata Kibil
Images: Shutterstock/Irtsya

INTRODUCTION

Kindness (noun):

The quality of being friendly, generous, and considerate.

"he thanked them for their kindness and support"

Kindness doesn't have to involve a radical overhaul of your life. You don't need to sell all your worldly goods and go overseas to dedicate your life to a worthy cause, just the smallest acts of kindness that you can easily weave into your everyday life can make a real difference. That little compliment given to a colleague, words of appreciation for your partner, encouraging a friend in need, or making an effort for a stranger can all turn around someone's day for the better. Sometimes it's the smallest things that mean the most.

Everyday Kindness brings you ideas on how you can make kindness a daily habit, with suggestions for random acts of kindness along with inspiring quotes to motivate you to be more compassionate. In being kinder to others, not only do we help to build up trust, community, and empathy within society, we increase our own happiness levels. Kindness is reciprocal, so what we give we will one day get back in return. Furthermore, research has shown that altruistic behavior releases endorphins in the brain and therefore boosts our own feelings of wellbeing.

When dedicating to being kind to others, it's important not to miss out one incredibly important person…you. You know the saying "to love others, you must first love yourself" and the same goes for kindness. In order to be able to be genuinely kind to others, you need to first be kind to yourself. Self-care is an incredibly important aspect of forging and maintaining a life filled with kind acts.

Just one kind act a day has the power to turn a life around, so use this book as your guide, inspiration, and motivation to embrace a year of kind living.

"Be kind, for everyone you meet is fighting a hard battle."

– PLATO

"One kind word can warm three winter months."

– JAPANESE PROVERB

PAY FOR A STRANGER

Today if you're in a store, or buying a coffee, pay for the person behind you. Be sure to keep the gesture an anonymous one, perhaps with a cheery "have a good day!" message that you could ask the person behind the counter to convey to your lucky recipient.

"If you want others to be happy, practice compassion. If you want to be happy, practice compassion."

– DALAI LAMA

"Don't wait for people
to be friendly,
show them how."

- UNKNOWN

EAT WELL

One of the simplest ways to be kind to yourself is to eat well.
Be conscious of what you consume and your body will thank
you for it.

"Be kinder to
yourself. And then
let your kindness
flood the world."

– PEMA CHODRON

"Those who bring sunshine to the lives of others cannot keep it from themselves."

– J.M. BARRIE

LET THEM KNOW YOU CARE

Write your partner a list of things you love about them. Whilst it may feel overly slushy, this kind of positive reinforcement is incredibly good for your relationship. It'll serve as a reminder to you of why you love them as well as making them feel all warm and fuzzy inside!

"There is nothing more truly artistic than to love people."

– VINCENT VAN GOGH

"A good character is the best tombstone. Those who loved you and were helped by you will remember you when forget-me-nots have withered. Carve your name on hearts, not on marble."

– CHARLES H. SPURGEON

BE POLITE

Hold the door open for the person behind you, let someone go in front of you in a line…small gestures such as these add up to create an enveloping attitude of kindness.

"Life's most persistent and nagging question is 'What are you doing for others?'"

– MARTIN LUTHER KING JR.

"How beautiful
a day can be,
when kindness
touches it!"

– GEORGE ELLISTON

"Kind words are short and easy to speak, but their echoes are truly endless."

– MOTHER TERESA

MEET FACE-TO-FACE

Instead of automatically texting or emailing, take time to connect with people on a face-to-face level. Give your time over to them fully, be genuinely attentive instead of squeezing them in and rushing off because you're in a hurry.

DO NOT COMPARE YOURSELF TO OTHERS

People who are truly kind to themselves never compare themselves to others. We are all on our own journey, fighting our own battles, with our own individual set of strengths and weaknesses. We are all good at different things and we all have different ambitions, motivations, and priorities in life.

"If your compassion does
not include yourself,
it is incomplete. "

– JACK KORNFIELD

"There is no exercise better
for the heart than reaching
down and lifting people up."

– JOHN HOLMES

SAY SORRY

…You know who to. Don't hold onto grudges or petty
resentments. Let them go and feel lighter in the process.

"Those best parts of a good life: little, nameless, unremembered acts of kindness and love."

– WILLIAM WORDSWORTH

"Too often we underestimate the power of a touch, a smile, a kind word, a listening ear, an honest compliment, or the smallest act of caring, all of which have the potential to turn a life around."

– LEO BUSCAGLIA

PRAISE A COLLEAGUE

Praise someone at work for a job well done. Try to do this when there are other people around to hear—extra points if you can do this in front of his/her boss!

"Perhaps you will forget tomorrow the kind words you say today, but the recipient may cherish them over a lifetime."

– DALE CARNEGIE

"Kindness is the twin sister of joy— we cannot have one without the other."

– HEATHER SHORE

"Three things in human life are important: the first is to be kind; the second is to be kind; and the third is to be kind."

– HENRY JAMES

"Be kind to unkind
people—they need
it the most."

– ASHLEIGH BRILLIANT

MAKE YOUR OWN MANTRAS

Write a list of life-affirming, positive statements to repeat to yourself whenever you are feeling inadequate or in need of a boost. You can adapt these to your own personal preferences and circumstances, but affirmations such as "I am enough," "I deserve happiness," and "I am worthy of all the kindness that comes my way" may be useful starting points.

"If the words you spoke
appeared on your
skin, would you still be
beautiful?"

– AULIQ ICE

CARVE OUT TIME FOR YOURSELF

Every day make sure you take time out for yourself to do something that brings you joy, whether it's a craft, a hobby, painting, reading, or just sitting in peace for five minutes.

"Give yourself some kindness today until you're filled and pass it on."

– LORI HIL

"Be kind to others,
so that you may learn
the secret art of being
kind to yourself."

– PARAMAHANSA YOGANANDA

"If in our daily life we can smile, if we can be peaceful and happy, not only we, but everyone will profit from it. This is the most basic kind of peace work."

– THICH NHAT HANH

"The words of kindness
are more healing to a
drooping heart than
balm or honey."

– SARAH FIELDING

GIVE A STRANGER A GIFT

Leave a gift for someone in a random public place. It's a good idea to drop this in a spot where people actually stop and sit, such as a bus stop or in a café, so people don't just hurriedly walk past oblivious to your offering.

DON'T JUDGE

The more you judge others, the more harshly you tend to judge yourself, so nobody wins from taking this particular standpoint in life. Remember you don't know other people's stories and battles and you're in no position to judge anyway.

"Through lovingkindness,
everyone and everything can
flower again from within."

– SHARON SALZBERG

"When you are kind to someone in trouble, you hope they'll remember and be kind to someone else. And it'll become like a wildfire."

– WHOOPI GOLDBERG

FORGIVE YOURSELF

We all make mistakes. Instead of dwelling on them, just resolve to do better in the future and move on.

"Do not speak badly of yourself. For the Warrior within hears your words and is lessened by them."

– DAVID GEMMELL

"And in spite of the fancies of youth, there's nothing so kingly as kindness, and nothing so royal as truth."

– ALICE CARY

STAND UP FOR SOMEONE

If someone in a vulnerable position is being bullied or talked down to, stand up for them. Speak out and protect them from unkind words or actions.

"A kind and
compassionate act is
often its own reward."

– WILLIAM JOHN BENNETT

SHARE

Very different from giving away things you no longer need, sharing is about giving away a little of something that is meaningful to you, whether it be half of your lunch, your favorite dress you could loan to a friend for a special occasion, or even words of advice.

"When you are kind
to others, it not only
changes you, it changes
the world."

– HAROLD KUSHNER

"One of the most difficult things to give away is kindness; it usually comes back to you."

– UNKNOWN

TREAT YOURSELF

If you get a promotion at work, meet a deadline, do something around the house that's been on your to-do list for ages…treat yourself. However minor your accomplishment may seem, treat yourself—whether in the form of a slice of cake, an item of clothing you've been coveting, or a coffee with a friend. Whatever makes you happy and positively reinforces your actions.

"The first rule of
kindness is to be kind
to yourself."

– BRYANT MCGILL

COMMENT ON A BLOG

If you have enjoyed reading a blog, leave a positive comment.

"For beautiful eyes, look for the good in others; for beautiful lips, speak only words of kindness; and for poise, walk with the knowledge that you are never alone."

– AUDREY HEPBURN

"Compassion isn't about solutions. It's about giving all the love that you've got."

– CHERYL STRAYED,
TINY BEAUTIFUL THINGS

"If we all do one random act of kindness daily, we might just set the world in the right direction."

– MARTIN KORNFELD

EMBRACE THE GOOD

Studies have shown that we subconsciously self-sabotage what we think we don't deserve, so if you don't think you are worthy of good things you won't accept them into your life. Tell yourself each day that you deserve all the positivity that comes your way. Be kind to yourself by embracing the good stuff.

"You can't live a perfect day without doing something for someone who will never be able to repay you."

– JOHN WOODEN

THE GIFT OF MUSIC

Make a playlist for a friend who needs cheering up. They'll know you've put time, effort, and thought into this and that knowledge will make them smile every time they listen to it.

"Kindness is the language which the deaf can hear and the blind can see."

– MARK TWAIN

"If your words are soft
and sweet, they won't
be as hard to swallow if
you have to eat them."

– UNKNOWN

PARK AND WALK

Park at the opposite end of the parking lot from the store, that way you'll give yourself some exercise as well as leaving nearer spaces free for those who may really need them.

"No act of kindness, no matter how small, is ever wasted."

– AESOP

"Kindness in words creates confidence. Kindness in thinking creates profoundness. Kindness in giving creates love."

– LAO TZU

COMPLIMENT

Make the effort to genuinely compliment at least three people—today and every day. Focus on things as trivial as a new haircut, through to character traits and achievements.

"Kindness is not a business. True kindness expects nothing in return and should never act with conditions."

– RAY T. BENNETT

"The dew of compassion
is a tear."

– LORD BYRON

"One can pay back the loan of gold, but one dies forever in debt to those who are kind."

– MALAYAN PROVERB

EXPRESS YOUR LOVE

Try saying "I love you" to friends and family a little more often.

"What wisdom can you find
that is greater than kindness?"

– JEAN-JACQUES ROUSSEAU

ACCEPT YOURSELF

The kindest thing you can do for yourself is to accept yourself for who you really are, faults and all. You will never be perfect, you can't be right all of the time, and you will not succeed in everything you do. But you are you, and that is enough.

"Be gentle first
with yourself if you
wish to be gentle
with others."

— LAMA YESHE

"There is nothing more beautiful than someone who goes out of their way to make life beautiful for others."

– MANDY HALE

"It's cool
to be kind."

– UNKNOWN

ADOPT A PET

Visit your local dog or cat rescue center and adopt an animal in need. Your kindness will be paid back tenfold by the love and joy a pet will bring into your life.

"It is the characteristic of the magnanimous man to ask no favor but to be ready to do kindness to others."

– ARISTOTLE

"We rise by lifting others."

— ROBERT INGERSOLL

EXPRESS YOUR GRATITUDE

Perhaps someone working in a store or restaurant has been really helpful to you, or maybe they have a really great manner with the public. Instead of just thinking it, tell them. Even small expressions of gratitude can make someone's day.

SPARE CHANGE?

Why not tape it to a parking meter for the next person.

"We don't have to engage
in grand, heroic actions to
participate in the process
of change. Small acts, when
multiplied by millions of people,
can transform the world."

– HOWARD ZINN

PLAN A STREET PARTY

This is a great way to do something for a number of people at the same time. It's a way of including more isolated neighbors, introducing people, and creating a happy community environment. Neighbors young and old will enjoy the chance to celebrate and socialize with one another.

"Kindness is doing what
you can, where you are,
with what you have."

– UNKNOWN

"Self-compassion is simply giving
the same kindness to ourselves
that we would give to others."

– CHRISTOPHER GERMER

DATE YOURSELF

Be kind to you. Take yourself off on a date to the theater, out for a meal, or treat yourself to a spa day.

"When a woman becomes her own best friend life is easier."

– DIANE VON FURSTENBERG

"Kindness is like snow—it beautifies everything it covers."

– KAHLIL GIBRAN

"A tree is known by its fruit; a man by his deeds. A good deed is never lost; he who sows courtesy reaps friendship, and he who plants kindness gathers love."

– SAINT BASIL

DO SOMEONE'S SHOPPING

Offer to shop for a homebound friend or neighbor. A little goes a long way for people unable to leave the house and be as agile and independent as they would like to be.

"A warm smile is the universal language of kindness."

– WILLIAM ARTHUR WARD

"Goodness is about character—integrity, honesty, kindness, generosity, moral courage, and the like. More than anything else, it is about how we treat other people."

– DENNIS PRAGER

SEND POSTCARDS

Find postcards with appropriate pictures on for various friends and drop them a random note just to thank them for being such a good friend.

"Forget injuries; never forget kindness."

– CONFUCIUS

"Do all the good you can.
By all the means you can. In all the
ways you can. In all the places you
can. At all the times you can. To
all the people you can. As long as
ever you can."

– JOHN WESLEY

"Every sunrise is an invitation for us to arise and brighten someone's day."

— RICHELLE E. GOODRICH

"The smallest
act of kindness
is worth more
than the grandest
intention."

– OSCAR WILDE

"By a sweet tongue and kindness, you can drag an elephant with a hair."

– PERSIAN PROVERB

"The way you speak to others can offer them joy, happiness, self-confidence, hope, trust, and enlightenment."

– THICH NHAT HANH

STOP COMPLAINING

Try to go a whole week without complaining about anything, and note the effect it has both on you and the people surrounding you. It will be more difficult than you think, but also more rewarding than you ever thought possible.

"It's easy to hate, it takes strength to be gentle and kind."

– THE SMITHS

VOLUNTEER

Volunteer to help others in need, perhaps at a homeless shelter serving meals or find an organization that matches your concerns and passions.

"If those who owe us nothing gave us nothing, how poor we would be."

– ANTONIO PORCHIA

"Those who make compassion an essential part of their lives find the joy of life. Kindness deepens the spirit and produces rewards that cannot be completely explained in words."

– ROBERT J. FUREY

GIVE BLOOD

You could be helping someone in a life-threatening situation.

"How do we change the world? One random act of kindness at a time."

– MORGAN FREEMAN

QUIT THE CRITICAL SELF TALK

Your niggling inner voice can be your worst critic, undermining your achievements and belittling your character. As these critical thoughts arise, replace each one with a positive statement about yourself.

"Put down the
bat and pick up
a feather, give
yourself a break."

– UNKNOWN

HUG

Give more hugs! According to scientific research, hugging makes us healthier, happier, and more resilient.

"Get out of your head and into your heart. Think less. Feel more."

– OSHO

"Kindness is more important than wisdom, and the recognition of this is the beginning of wisdom."

– THEODORE ISAAC RUBIN

"By swallowing evil words unsaid, no one has ever harmed his stomach."

– WINSTON CHURCHILL

"Be the person that makes others feel special. Be known for your kindness and grace."

– UNKNOWN

"Even when you are hurt
being kind to others will
help the hurt."

– CATHERINE PULSIFER

WISH THEM LUCK!

Buy a dozen lottery tickets and hand them out to strangers on the street.

HAVE COMPASSION

If someone has done something you don't like or is being rude to you, instead of going on the defensive try to be compassionate toward their situation. Tell yourself maybe they're just having a bad day. Perhaps all they need is to hear a kind word from you and they'll do a U-turn on their attitude—you may be surprised at the results if you try this one!

"I have no desire to move mountains, construct monuments, or leave behind in my wake material evidence of my existence. But in the final recollection, if the essence of my being has caused a smile to have appeared upon your face or a touch of joy within your heart...then in living—I have made my mark."

– THOMAS L. ODEM, JR.

"One person can make a difference, and everyone should try."

– JOHN F. KENNEDY

"There are no traffic jams when you go the extra mile."

– KENNETH MCFARLAND

LEND AN ELDERLY PERSON A HAND

Helping someone less agile than yourself across the road, or to reach something from a high shelf in the supermarket is no great effort for you but this simple act of kindness could really make a difference to someone else's day.

"Beginning today, treat everyone you meet as if they were going to be dead by midnight. Extend to them all the care, kindness and understanding you can muster, and do it with no thought of any reward. Your life will never be the same again."

– OG MANDINO

"True beauty is born through our actions and aspirations and in the kindness we offer to others."

– ALEK WEK

SOOTHE YOURSELF

After a hard day be sure to look after yourself: Take a long soak in the bath, read a book, or listen to music. Whatever soothes you and restores your soul.

"You will never speak
to anyone more than
you speak to yourself
in your head. Be kind
to yourself."

– UNKNOWN

TAKE A BREAK FROM TECHNOLOGY

One very simple way to be kinder to yourself is to take a break from technology. Log off from social media, where you're pretty likely to be comparing yourself and your own life to an inevitably filtered, edited, and unrealistically curated version of someone else's. Stop chasing virtual "likes" for a while and you may just start to like yourself and your life a little more.

"Do not be a harsh judge of yourself, without kindness toward ourself, we cannot love the world."

– BUDDHA

"A single act of kindness throws out roots in all directions, and the roots spring up and make new trees."

– AMELIA EARHART

"Be kind whenever possible. It is always possible."

– DALAI LAMA

PUT PEN TO PAPER

Write a letter to someone who has made a big difference in your life, perhaps a teacher or a former boss, to express how grateful you are for their support, guidance, or kindness. Tell them how glad you are that they have been a part of your life and what a positive effect they have had.

"The way you speak to others can offer them joy, happiness, self-confidence, hope, trust, and enlightenment."

– THICH NHAT HANH

"Real generosity is doing
something nice for someone
who will never find out."

– FRANK A. CLARK

"You cannot do a kindness too soon, for you never know how soon it will be too late."

– RALPH WALDO EMERSON

GO ON A FIRST-AID COURSE

Learn CPR and you could save someone's life.

"Kindness, like
a boomerang,
always returns."

– UNKNOWN

"Love only grows by sharing. You can only have more for yourself by giving it away to others."

– BRIAN TRACY

SWITCH THE DIRECTION OF A NEGATIVE CONVERSATION

If the people you're chatting with are gossiping about someone or complaining, bring the conversation around to something positive. Mention something good the person they're gossiping about has done, for example. Be the one to chime in with a kind word.

"Kindness does
wonderful things
to a face."

– DIXIE DOYLE

"You can be rich in spirit, kindness, love and all those things that you can't put a dollar sign on."

– DOLLY PARTON

MAKE SOMEONE FEEL WELCOME

If you have a new neighbor, bake them a cake or take them flowers to welcome them to the street. If you have a new colleague at work, make them a coffee and take the time to introduce yourself. If there's a new member of a club you belong to, make the effort to engage with them. Whatever the arena, make newcomers feel welcome.

"I want to be the kind of person that kind people like and want to be like."

— JAROD KINTZ

"He who sees a need and waits to be asked for help is as unkind as if he had refused it."

– DANTE

"Life is made up, not of great sacrifices or duties, but of little things, in which smiles and kindness, and small obligations given habitually, are what preserve the heart and secure comfort."

– HUMPHRY DAVY

NURTURE YOUR DREAMS

People who are kind to themselves honor their dreams. They take them seriously and don't brush them aside or label them as pipedreams. Take your dreams seriously by making plans and turning them into attainable step-by-step goals.

"Be kind to yourself
so you can be happy
enough to be kind
to the world."

– MISHA COLLINS

STOP WORRYING ABOUT WHAT OTHERS THINK OF YOU

Instead worry about what you think. Listen to your own inner voice.

"The only people with whom you should try to get even are those who have helped you."

– JOHN E. SOUTHARD

"There is overwhelming evidence that the higher the level of self-esteem, the more likely one will be to treat others with respect, kindness, and generosity."

– NATHANIEL BRANDEN

COLLECT DONATIONS

Volunteer to collect unwanted items from friends and neighbors and deliver them to local charities or shelters. Take any food they can spare to food banks. This is a great way to encourage others to be kind and charitable alongside you.

"Good nature will always
supply the absence
of beauty; but beauty
cannot supply the
absence of good nature."

– JOSEPH ADDISON

"Wherever there is a
human being, there is an
opportunity for kindness."

– SENECA

REACH OUT...

...to a friend in need. Call them, send them a text message, or flower...Just let them know you are thinking of them.

"The very nature of kindness is to spread. If you are kind to others, today they will be kind to you, and tomorrow to somebody else."

– SRI CHINMOY

STOP AND TALK

Make the effort to stop and talk to a homeless person today.
Listen to their story.

"Always be a little
kinder than necessary."

– J.M. BARRIE

ACCEPT OTHER PEOPLE'S KINDNESS

As well as being kind yourself, it's important to accept kindness from others. There needs to be this balance to maintain the reciprocal cycle of kindness.

"Take a rest; a field
that has rested gives a
beautiful crop."

– OVID

"Our human compassion binds us the one to the other–not in pity or patronizingly, but as human beings who have learnt how to turn our common suffering into hope for the future."

– NELSON MANDELA

"My religion is very
simple. My religion
is kindness."

– DALAI LAMA

BE PATIENT

We all lead busy lives, but getting impatient isn't going to make that line go down any faster, the traffic light turn green, or the bus come any quicker.

"Nothing can make our life, or the lives of other people, more beautiful than perpetual kindness."

– LEO TOLSTOY

"A kind gesture can reach a wound that only compassion can heal."

– STEVE MARABOLI

"The end result of kindness is that it draws people to you."

– ANITA RODDICK

SOCIAL NICETIES

If you're at a party or similar social situation and you see someone alone and looking awkward, go over and strike up a conversation with them.

"There is no effect more disproportionate to its cause than the happiness bestowed by a small compliment."

– ROBERT BRAULT

"Human kindness has never weakened the stamina or softened the fiber of a free people. A nation does not have to be cruel to be tough."

– FRANKLIN D. ROOSEVELT

"A spark of kindness
starts a fire of love."

- UNKNOWN

ACKNOWLEDGE YOUR FEELINGS

Being kind to yourself means allowing yourself to feel whatever it is you're feeling. Recognize that your feelings and emotions are valid and give yourself permission to experience them without judgment.

"Compassionate action has to start with ourselves. If we are willing to stand fully in our own shoes and never give up on ourselves, then we will be able to put ourselves in the shoes of others and never give up on them."

– PEMA CHODRON

"Every act of kindness grows the spirit and strengthens the soul."

– UNKNOWN

"One who knows how to show and to accept kindness will be a friend better than any possession."

– SOPHOCLES

HELP A COLLEAGUE

If you see a co-worker struggling with a project or a deadline offer to help them out. Or if it's not in an area of your expertise, make them coffee and offer up encouraging words.

LISTEN

Don't just talk at people today, instead really listen to their responses and what they have to say. Making a conscious effort to do this will teach you how much you filter out and how often you do not give people your full attention. We're all guilty of it.

SHOW YOURSELF LOVING COMPASSION

Envisage a loved one feeling hurt or upset. Imagine what you would say to them, how you would comfort them, reassure them, care for them and make them feel better. Summon up these feelings of compassion and now direct them toward yourself.

"How you treat yourself is how you are inviting the world to treat you."

– UNKNOWN

"Today, give a stranger
one of your smiles.
It might be the only
sunshine he sees all day."

– H. JACKSON BROWN JR.

BE OPTIMISTIC

For kindness to come from the heart, to be truly genuine rather than arising from a sense of duty, you need to have an optimistic mindset, to be able to see the good in life and in people. The best way to cultivate optimism is through focusing on the positive aspects of your life and by being grateful for all that you have. It takes practice!

"I always prefer to believe the best of everybody, it saves so much trouble."

– RUDYARD KIPLING

PICK UP LITTER

If you see garbage left on the pavements, pick it up as you walk. Make the places you travel through better for you having been there.

"Do your little bit of good where you are; it's those little bits of good put together that overwhelm the world."

– DESMOND TUTU

LEAVE GOOD REVIEWS

We tend to be more willing to complain about bad service than compliment good. When you've had positive experiences, be sure to leave good reviews of that business on their website.

"Kindness can transform someone's dark moment with a blaze of light. You'll never know how much your caring matters. Make a difference for another today."

– AMY LEIGH MERCREE

"A person who does
things that count
doesn't usually stop
to count them."

– UNKNOWN

"Kind hearts are the gardens,
Kind thoughts are the roots,
Kind words are the blossoms,
Kind deeds are the fruits."

– KIRPAL SINGH

MIND YOUR MANNERS

Saying "please" and "thank you" is the simplest way to improve all your interactions with others.

"Kindness is the velvet
of social intercourse."

– JAMES L. GORDON

"As perfume to
the flower, so is
kindness to speech."

– KATHERINE FRANCKE

"It is the characteristic of the magnanimous man to ask no favor but to be ready to do kindness to others."

– ARISTOTLE

"Admire someone else's beauty without questioning your own."

– UNKNOWN

GIVE YOURSELF RECOGNITION

Don't skip over your achievements, dwell on them. When you've accomplished a goal or done something you're proud of, stop and acknowledge it. Give yourself a pat on the back and congratulate yourself.

"Be kind to yourself this evening. Buy something for yourself. Treat yourself to a meal. Look in the mirror and give yourself a smile."

– YOKO ONO

"There is a very real relationship,
both quantitatively and
qualitatively, between what you
contribute and what you get out
of this world."

– OSCAR HAMMERSTEIN II

MAKE SOMEONE LAUGH

Laughter really is the greatest gift, so make the effort to make someone laugh today. Tell a joke, recall a funny anecdote, send a link to an amusing article…do whatever it takes to raise a giggle.

"It is one of the great secrets of life that those things which are most worth doing, we do for others."

– LEWIS CARROLL

"Let us practice random kindness and acts of senseless beauty to all we meet."

– PAUL KELLER

SEND A
VALENTINE'S CARD...

...in August.

"We should give as we would receive: cheerfully, quickly, and without hesitation; for there is no grace in a benefit that sticks to the fingers."

– SENECA

"You can accomplish by kindness what you cannot by force."

– PUBLILIUS SYRUS

"I feel the capacity to care is the thing which gives life its deepest significance."

— PABLO CASALS

OFFER YOUR COMPANY...

…To an elderly relative or neighbor who may be feeling isolated. Just offering up ten minutes of your time to go and have a cup of tea and a chat with them could really make a difference to their day.

"No act of kindness is too small. The gift of kindness may start as a small ripple that over time can turn into a tidal wave affecting the lives of many."

– KEVIN HEATH

A FREE LUNCH

Make yourself two lunches and give one away to a colleague.

"Kindness is the sunshine in which virtue grows."

– ROBERT GREEN INGERSOLL

"Sure the world breeds
monsters, but kindness
grows just as wild..."

— MARY KARR

"One man practicing
kindness in the wilderness
is worth all the temples
this world pulls."

– JACK KEROUAC

BACK DOWN

You don't have to become a doormat to be kind, but where possible try giving someone the benefit of the doubt and back down from an argument.

"The best way to knock the chip off your neighbor's shoulder is to pat him on the back."

– UNKNOWN

"Men are cruel, but
man is kind."

– RABINDRANATH TAGORE

"Kindness is in our power, even when fondness is not."

– SAMUEL JOHNSON

GET MORE SLEEP

Take the opportunity of an early night when you can. A good night's sleep improves all aspects of life!

"Talk to yourself like you would to someone you love."

– BRENÉ BROWN

SPREAD INSPIRING MESSAGES

Scribble positive words and inspiring messages on Post-Its and stick them up around your workplace. You may just give your co-workers a boost when they most need it, or at least make them smile.

"Everywhere you go, leave a glitter trail of kindness behind you."

– UNKNOWN

WRITE YOUR BUCKET LIST

Write a list of all the things you would most like to do in your lifetime. By writing them down you are acknowledging the fact that your hopes and dreams matter.

"It is an absolute human certainty that no one can know his own beauty or perceive a sense of his own worth until it has been reflected back to him in the mirror of another loving, caring human being."

– JOHN JOSEPH POWELL

"Great opportunities to help others seldom come, but small ones surround us every day."

– SALLY KOCH

BUY A HOMELESS PERSON A HOT DRINK OR MEAL

You don't have to spend a lot of money to provide some nutrition and comfort where it's most needed.

"The kindness planned
for tomorrow doesn't
count for today."

– UNKNOWN

"Never doubt that a small group of thoughtful, committed citizens can change the world. Indeed, it is the only thing that ever has."

– MARGARET MEAD

"Kindness—that simple word. To be kind—it covers everything, to my mind. If you're kind that's it."

– ROALD DAHL

"I've learned that people will forget what you said, people will forget what you did, but people will never forget how you made them feel."

–MAYA ANGELOU

BE FRIENDLY

You don't have to be a raging extrovert to be friendly to those around you, just a smile and some small talk can make a big difference. Being pleasant to people, showing an interest in them, and paying them a little attention could drastically improve their day.

"We may never truly know the reach of an act of kindness or the mark that it leaves on a life."

– TOPAZ

"Kind words will unlock
an iron door."

– TURKISH PROVERB

ACCENTUATE THE POSITIVE

Don't fall into the trap of becoming your own worst critic. Write a list of all your positive character traits and when your self-esteem is low refer back to this list and focus on your good points.

"Be kind to yourself as you proceed along this journey. This kindness, in itself, is a means of awakening the spark of love within you and helping others to discover that spark within themselves."

– TSOKNYI RINPOCHE

"Kindness in women, not their beauteous looks, shall win my love."

– WASHINGTON IRVING

TELL THE TRUTH

Don't be tempted to tell white lies to protect someone's feelings. Your intentions may be worthy but the truth is always kinder in the long run.

"There is no wrong way to perform an act of kindness."

– CATHERINE RYAN HYDE

"How far that little candle
throws his beams!

So shines a good deed in
a naughty world."

– WILLIAM SHAKESPEARE

USE YOUR SKILLS TO HELP OTHERS

If you're a skilled cook, make someone a meal—either deliver it to their doorstep or invite them over for dinner; if you're a good writer offer to read over a friend's assignment or work presentation; if you're artistic you could help someone design and decorate their new home; if you're a fitness guru offer to help a friend trying to lose weight…You just need to tap into your skillset and find ways to spread the love.

"When you carry out acts of kindness you get a wonderful feeling inside. It is as though something inside your body responds and says, yes, this is how I ought to feel."

– HAROLD KUSHNER

"Kindness is the only service that will stand the storm of life and not wash out. It will wear well and will be remembered long after the prism of politeness or the complexion of courtesy has faded away."

– ABRAHAM LINCOLN

ACKNOWLEDGE PEOPLE WHEN THEY WALK INTO THE ROOM...

…It only takes a moment to look up and say hello.

"Acts of kindness are the
blossoms of the soul."

– ANTHONY DOUGLAS WILLIAMS

TEACH CHILDREN TO BE KIND

Around the dinner table ask the members of your household what they did today and talk about any acts of kindness they may have performed. Tell them what you did to be kind and teach them by example. Put a lot of value on kindness, and give a lot of praise for any thoughtful acts.

"Teaching a child not to step on a caterpillar is as valuable to the child as it is to the caterpillar."

– BRADLEY MILLER

"Kindness is more than deeds. It is an attitude, an expression, a look, a touch. It is anything that lifts another person."

– PLATO

"You yourself, as much as anybody in the entire universe, deserve your love and affection."

– BUDDHA

PRAISE YOURSELF

Each night note down everything you have achieved during the day, no matter how small, and mentally praise yourself for your day's accomplishments.

"If you wouldn't say it
to a friend, don't say it
to yourself."

– JANE TRAVIS

"Think of giving not as a
duty but as a privilege."

– JOHN D. ROCKEFELLER

"Be somebody who
makes everybody feel like
a somebody."

– ROBBY NOVAK

BUY UNEXPECTED GIFTS

Treat loved ones to unexpected presents. They don't have to be expensive, just thoughtful and a surprise. You'll make their day when they're least expecting it!

"Kind deeds often come back to the givers in fairer shapes than they go."

– LOUISA M. ALCOTT

FLOWERBOMB YOUR STREETS

Drop wildflower seeds on any neglected public ground and watch your neighborhood bloom as Spring comes around.

"Be the reason someone believes in the goodness of people."

– KAREN SALAWOHN

BE A COURTEOUS DRIVER

Give way to someone if they appear to be in a rush. Help make their journey that little bit less stressful.

"Be silly.

Be honest.

Be kind."

– RALPH WALDO EMERSON

"So many gods, so many creeds,
So many paths that wind and wind,
While just the art of being kind
Is all the sad world needs."

– ELLA WHEELER WILCOX

"What sunshine is to flowers, smiles are to humanity. These are but trifles, to be sure; but scattered along life's pathway, the good they do is inconceivable."

– JOSEPH ADDISON

"Give out what you most want to come back."

– ROBIN S. SHARMA

"We think too much and feel too little. More than machinery, we need humanity. More than cleverness, we need kindness and gentleness."

– CHARLIE CHAPLIN

MAKE THAT PHONE CALL

We all have people we haven't seen in a while who we keep meaning to call. Do it today and make their day. Whether it's a relative or an old friend, perhaps someone who moved jobs or out of your neighborhood so you lost touch, they will be pleased to hear from you.

"What I call the depth of generosity is when people are very fond of giving away what they need most themselves."

– OSCAR WILDE

"When I was young, I admired clever people. Now that I am old, I admire kind people."

– ABRAHAM JOSHUA HESCHEL

TREAT THE KIDS

Take a group of children you know on a special trip,
perhaps to the zoo or a fair, a petting farm, or simply
for a play at the park.

"Kindness is just love with
its work boots on."

– UNKNOWN

"Life is an echo. What you send out, comes back. What you sow, you reap. What you give, you get. What you see in others, exists in you."

– ZIG ZIGLAR

"Carry out a random act of kindness, with no expectation of reward, safe in the knowledge that one day someone might do the same for you."

– PRINCESS DIANA

DONATE MAGAZINES

Take magazines you've read along to waiting rooms in your local hospital or doctor's surgery.

"Kindness is the golden
chain by which society
is bound together."

– JOHANN WOLFGANG VON GOETHE

"Be careful how you are talking to yourself because you are listening."

– LISA M. HAYES

COMPLIMENT YOURSELF

Look and the mirror and think of three positive things to say about yourself. Practice this daily for greater self-acceptance and all-round wellbeing.

"Giving yourself some loving attention isn't selfish—it's sensible. If you feel loved and cherished (even if it's only by yourself) you'll have more love to give others."

– PENELOPE QUEST

DISCOVER YOUR STRENGTHS

Focus on the things you're good at rather than worrying about your weaknesses. Engage your natural strengths on a daily basis—whether at work or through hobbies and extra-curricular activities—for greater levels of confidence and contentment.

"We are all of us stars and we all deserve to twinkle."

– MARILYN MONROE

"When words are both true
and kind, they can change
the world."

– BUDDHA

"Constant kindness can accomplish much. As the sun melts ice, kindness causes misunderstanding, mistrust, and hostility to evaporate."

– ALBERT SCHWEITZER

ENCOURAGE YOUR CHILDREN TO DONATE

Give them a box each and ask them to collect together any toys or games that they no longer play with. Take them to a local thrift shop or children's charity together so the children get involved in the whole process of giving.

"Because that's what kindness is. It's not doing something for someone else because they can't, but because you can."

– ANDREW ISKANDER

"No one has ever become poor by giving."

– ANNE FRANK

GIVE PHOTOS AS UNEXPECTED GIFTS

When you have taken a flattering photo of somebody, print it out and give it to them.

"Unexpected kindness is the most powerful, least costly, and most underrated agent of human change."

– BOB KERREY

"Don't cast a shadow on anyone unless you're providing shade."

– TERRI GUILLEMETS

RELAX

Practice deep relaxation techniques, such as yogic breathing or engage in a mindfulness meditation (try an app like Headspace). Relaxing should feature on your to-do list just as prominently as all the errands and deadlines.

"As the rain falls on the just and unjust alike, let your heart be untroubled by judgments and let your kindness rain down on all."

– BUDDHA

TAKE CAKES INTO WORK

Share them out during coffee breaks and spread a little sugary love. For the more health conscious, substitute with fruit.

CREATE A TO-DO LIST OF ENJOYABLE ACTIVITIES...

…and pledge to do at least three of these each day. They can include anything from taking a walk in nature, reading, knitting, listening to music, exercising, or meditating. Anything that brings you joy or inspires you. When you make doing these part of your daily to-do list you're conditioning yourself to believe that you deserve to do what you enjoy, to treat yourself with kindness.

"When you recover or discover something that nourishes your soul and brings joy, care enough about yourself to make room for it in your life."

– JEAN SHINODA BOLEN

"Love and compassion are necessities, not luxuries. Without them, humanity cannot survive."

– DALAI LAMA

"A bit of fragrance always clings to the hand that gives roses."

– CHINESE PROVERB

HIDE NOTES...

…Maybe in your child's lunchbox, or a partner's coat pocket. Some words of encouragement, or a loving message to wish them a happy day is sure to make them smile.

"No one is useless in this world who lightens the burden of another."

— CHARLES DICKENS

"Guard well within yourself that treasure, kindness. Know how to give without hesitation, how to lose without regret, how to acquire without meanness."

– GEORGE SAND

CURB YOUR ANGER

Disengage from conflict wherever possible and try to keep angry thoughts and feelings in check. If you're feeling riled up about something, chances are you'll end up saying or doing something you'll regret. Before speaking or taking rash action, stop and count to ten.

"Treat everyone with politeness and kindness, not because they are nice, but because you are."

– ROY T. BENNETT

"Our days are happier
when we give people our
heart rather than a piece
of our mind."

– RITU GHATOUREY

SMILE

Smile as you chat to friends, smile at strangers you pass in the street, the people who serve you in shops or restaurants, colleagues across the office. Just smile!

"The shortest distance between two people is a smile."

– VICTOR BORGE

"A part of kindness consists in loving people more than they deserve."

– JOSEPH JOUBERT

DON'T PRACTICE CONDITIONAL KINDNESS

Be kind to everyone who crosses your path, not just those who you think deserve your kindness.

"Never look down on anybody unless you're helping him up."

– JESSE JACKSON

"In about the same degree
as you are helpful, you will
be happy."

– KARL REILAND

"Sometimes it's easy to lose faith in people. And sometimes one act of kindness is all it takes to give you hope again."

– RANDA ABDEL-FATTAH

LISTEN TO YOUR THOUGHTS

Spend some time in silent contemplation. Use this time to focus just on you, on your hopes and dreams, your thoughts and feelings. This could be in the form of meditation, or just quiet reflection. One of the kindest things you can do for yourself is to give airtime to your inner thoughts.

"Tenderness and
kindness are not signs of
weakness and despair, but
manifestations of strength
and resolution."

– KAHLIL GIBRAN

"When you can be the sunshine in someone's life, or the warm rain, why would you be the cold north wind?"

– ROBERT BRAULT

"Be kind to those that meet you as you rise, you may pass them again as you fall."

– IRISH PROVERB

TREAT YOUR PARTNER

Take them coffee in bed, cook them a delicious meal, write them a poem…It's amazing how easy it is to forget to be kind to those we love the most.

"Kindness makes
a fellow feel good
whether it's being done
to him or by him."

– FRANK A. CLARK

JUST SAY "NO"

It's so important to speak out if people are asking too much of you. Learn how to put your own needs first and say "no"— whether it be to an invitation for a social occasion when you're feeling exhausted, or another work project when you're already overloaded, or to a toxic person in your life.

"Genuine kindness is no ordinary act, but a gift of rare beauty."

– SYLVIA ROSSETTI

"Ask yourself: Have you been kind today? Make kindness your daily *modus operandi* and change your world."

– ANNIE LENNOX

GIVE AWAY YOUR FAVORITE BOOKS

Share the joy of a great read by giving away books you love.

"Remember there's no such thing as a small act of kindness. Every act creates a ripple with no logical end."

– SCOTT ADAMS

"The love, kindnesses, and value we have given authentically to others will be our remaining treasures at the end of life."

– STEVE BRUNKHORST

ORGANIZE A FUNDRAISING EVENT

Select a cause close to your heart and organize an event to raise money for it. This could be anything from an auction of promises to a comedy or quiz night.

"When we're kind to ourselves, we create a reservoir of compassion that we can extend to others."

– BRENÉ BROWN

ENGAGE IN REGULAR EXERCISE

In addition to the plethora of well-known health benefits, exercise can also be good for the brain, with scientific research suggesting that it can aid relaxation, improve cognitive function, reduce anxiety, and lower the risk of depression.

"The true meaning of life is to plant trees, under whose shade you do not expect to sit."

– NELSON HENDERSON

"Do all the good you can, and make as little fuss about it as possible."

– CHARLES DICKENS

"Kindness is always fashionable, and always welcome."

– AMELIA BARR

IMPROVE YOUR AREA

If there is any neglected wasteland in your neighborhood, why not plant a tree or some flowers? This is a really easy way to improve the look of an area. If the town you live in is in particular need of some TLC, consider starting a campaign and getting a group of volunteers together to plant flowers, do litter picks, etc.

"What this world needs is a new kind of army—the army of the kind."

– CLEVELAND AMORY

"Kindness has a beautiful way of reaching down into a weary heart and making it shine like the rising sun."

– UNKNOWN

SHOW AFFECTION

Express your love through hugs and kisses. A pat on the back, a rub of the shoulders, or any other gentle sign of affection will be appreciated.

"When we give cheerfully and accept gratefully, everyone is blessed."

– MAYA ANGELOU

"To err on the side
of kindness is seldom
an error."

– LIZ ARMBRUSTER

CHOOSE YOUR WORDS CAREFULLY

Pause before you speak. Everything that comes out of your mouth doesn't have to be all hearts and flowers, but try to only express thoughts, feelings, ideas, and opinions with positive intention.

"Never lose a chance of saying a kind word."

– WILLIAM MAKEPEACE THACKERAY

"The seeds of kindness that you plant today, will one day bloom in the heart of all that you touch."

– UNKNOWN

"The greatest good you can do for another is not just to share your riches but to reveal to him his own."

– BENJAMIN DISRAELI

BE A MENTOR

Volunteer to be a mentor, perhaps at a school for children who need extra guidance, or for a junior colleague or intern in your office. Use your skills and experience to help others.

"Every time you help
somebody stand
up you are helping
humanity rise."

– STEVE MARABOLI

"He who distributes the milk of human kindness cannot help but spill a little on himself."

– J.M. BARRIE

"Kind people are the
best kind of people."

– UNKNOWN

"In this life we cannot always do great things. But we can do small things with great love."

– MOTHER TERESA

BABYSIT

If you are friends or neighbors with any tired parents of young children, offer to babysit for them so they can have a well-deserved night out.

"Be nice to yourself. It's hard to be happy when someone is mean to you all the time."

– CHRISTINE ARYLO

STOP STRIVING FOR PERFECTION

Give yourself a break and ditch the illusion of perfection. We are all flawed and beating yourself up for not being perfect is going to have a detrimental impact on every aspect of your life. Love your imperfect self.

"What is fundamentally beautiful is compassion, for yourself and those around you. That kind of beauty enflames the heart and enchants the soul."

– LUPITA NYONG'O

BECOME AN ORGAN DONOR...

...And tell your family about it.

"Fashion your
life as a garland of
beautiful deeds."

– BUDDHA

SHOW THEM THE WAY

Give directions to a tourist who may be looking lost—don't wait for them to ask. Whilst you're at it, why not recommend them your favorite restaurant in the area.

"The everyday kindness
of the back roads more
than makes up for the
acts of greed in the
headlines."

– CHARLES KURALT

"Don't be yourself—be someone a little nicer."

– MIGNON MCLAUGHLIN

SEND A CARE PACKAGE...

...To a sick friend, or an elderly relative. Let them know you're thinking of them.

"Kindness is gladdening the hearts of those who are traveling the dark journey with us."

– HENRI-FREDERIC AMIEL

OFFER SHELTER

Keep umbrellas in the trunk of your car and hand them out to people who get caught without one on a rainy day.

"A kind heart is a
fountain of gladness,
making everything
in its vicinity freshen
into smiles."

– WASHINGTON IRVING

"Kindness gives birth
to kindness."

– SOPHOCLES

"To give pleasure
to a single heart by
a single act is better
than a thousand heads
bowing in prayer."

– MAHATMA GANDHI

INVITE SOMEONE TO DINNER…

…Maybe a lonely friend, someone who has just been through a breakup or difficult time in their life…anyone who would appreciate a little company and a good meal.

GIVE UP YOUR SEAT

If you're on a train or bus and someone looks like they could use a seat—perhaps they're pregnant or elderly—don't wait for someone else to get up. Offer them your seat instead.

"If a man be gracious and courteous to strangers, it shows he is a citizen of the world, and that his heart is no island cut off from other lands, but a continent that joins them."

– FRANCIS BACON

"One man cannot hold another man down in the ditch without remaining down in the ditch with him."

– BOOKER T. WASHINGTON

"Recompense injury with justice, and recompense kindness with kindness."

– CONFUCIUS

"To share often and much…
to know even one life has
breathed easier because you
have lived. This is to have
succeeded."

– RALPH WALDO EMERSON

ENGAGE WITH NATURAL BEAUTY

Take time out to immerse yourself in a natural environment. As well as having a positive impact on your own mood something as simple as a walk in woods could actually increase your capacity for kindness. Studies have shown that experiencing the beauty of nature increases positive emotions, which in turn leads to kindness.

"A kind word is like a Spring day."

– RUSSIAN PROVERB

"We make a living by what we get, but we make a life by what we give."

– WINSTON CHURCHILL

PUT YOUR PHONE DOWN

When someone walks into the room, put your phone away so you can communicate with them face-to-face. Several studies are now suggesting that the amount of time we spend engaging with technology instead of each other is having a detrimental effect on our ability to empathize.

"We cannot live only for ourselves. A thousand fibers connect us with our fellow men; and among those fibers, as sympathetic threads, our actions run as causes, and they come back to us as effects."

– HERMAN MELVILLE

"As we work to create light for others, we naturally light our own way."

– MARY ANNE RADMACHER

VISIT A NURSING HOME

Offer to read to or play a board game with a resident who doesn't get any visitors.

"We're here for a reason. I believe a bit of the reason is to throw little torches out to lead people through the dark."

– WHOOPI GOLDBERG

BUY A STORE GIFT CARD...

...And on your way out of the store hand it to someone walking in.

"When words are both
true and kind, they can
change the world."

– BUDDHA

BE ENCOURAGING

Become someone's cheerleader; a friend who wants to change jobs, get fit, leave a toxic relationship, start a business…whatever their goal, encourage them every step of the way.

"Choose being kind over being right and you will be right every time."

– RICHARD CARLSON

"Kindness can become its own motive. We are made kind by being kind."

– ERIC HOFFER

LEARN FROM OTHERS

Bring to mind the kindest people in your life. Think about how they act with others and try to emulate their behavior. It will soon become a natural habit for you, too.

"The world is changed by your example, not by your opinion."

– PAULO COELHO

"The great acts of love
are done by those who
are habitually performing
small acts of kindness."

– VICTOR HUGO

SEND A THOUGHTFUL NOTE

Send someone who you know is going through a hard time a card with a few well-chosen, thoughtful words.

"You will never have a completely bad day if you show kindness at least once."

– GREG HENRY QUINN

"It's a little embarrassing that after 45 years of research and study, the best advice I can give people is to be a little kinder to each other."

– ALDOUS HUXLEY

TREAT OTHERS HOW YOU WOULD LIKE TO BE TREATED YOURSELF

Keep this golden rule in mind in all your relationships, behavior, and interactions with others and you won't go far wrong when it comes to upping your kindness quota.

"In the long run, the
sharpest weapon of all is
a kind and gentle spirit."

– ANNE FRANK

"As long as you're breathing, it's never too late to do some good."

– MAYA ANGELOU

"When I am gone, I hope it can be said of me that I plucked a thistle and planted a flower wherever I thought a flower would grow."

– UNKNOWN